Yippee! It's spring in the Kingdom of Ying!

The striped bells of the tower begin to ring.

The polka-dot bullfrogs all start to sing.

The courteous cows push pigs on a swing.

The teeny-weeny raindrops whisper, "ping, ping, ping."

The very happy honeybees decide not to sting.

Two dogs make bouquets
from the daisies cats bring.

The rooster unwinds his great ball of string,

 8

sending his kite up in the air on a fling,

beckoning the blue jay to wave "Hi" with her wing,

bringing a smile to the face of the king.

For all of the land is loaded with zing—

what a wonderful, wonderful, wonderful thing!

-ing Word Family Riddles

Listen to the riddle sentences. Add the right letter or letters to the -ing sound to finish each one.

1 You should curtsy or bow when you greet the ___ing.

2 Early in the morning the birds like to ___ing.

3 My kite is attached to a long piece of _____ing.

4 Listen! Can you hear the telephone ___ing?

5 The winter is over. Now it is _____ing.

6 If you frighten a bee, it may try to ____ing.

7 We can tie this tire to a branch to make a great ____ing.

8 I've been invited to a party. What shall I ____ing?

9 The rubber band snapped with a __ing.

10 A duck can sleep with its head under its __ing.

> **Now make up some new riddle sentences using -ing**

-ing Cheer

Give a great holler, a cheer, a yell

For all of the words that we can spell

With an I, N, and G that make the sound –ing,

You'll find it in king and ring and sing.

Three little letters, that's all that we need

To make a whole family of words to read!

Make a list of other –ing words. Then use them in the cheer!